D1753321

WHO WORKS IN MY NEIGHBORHOOD

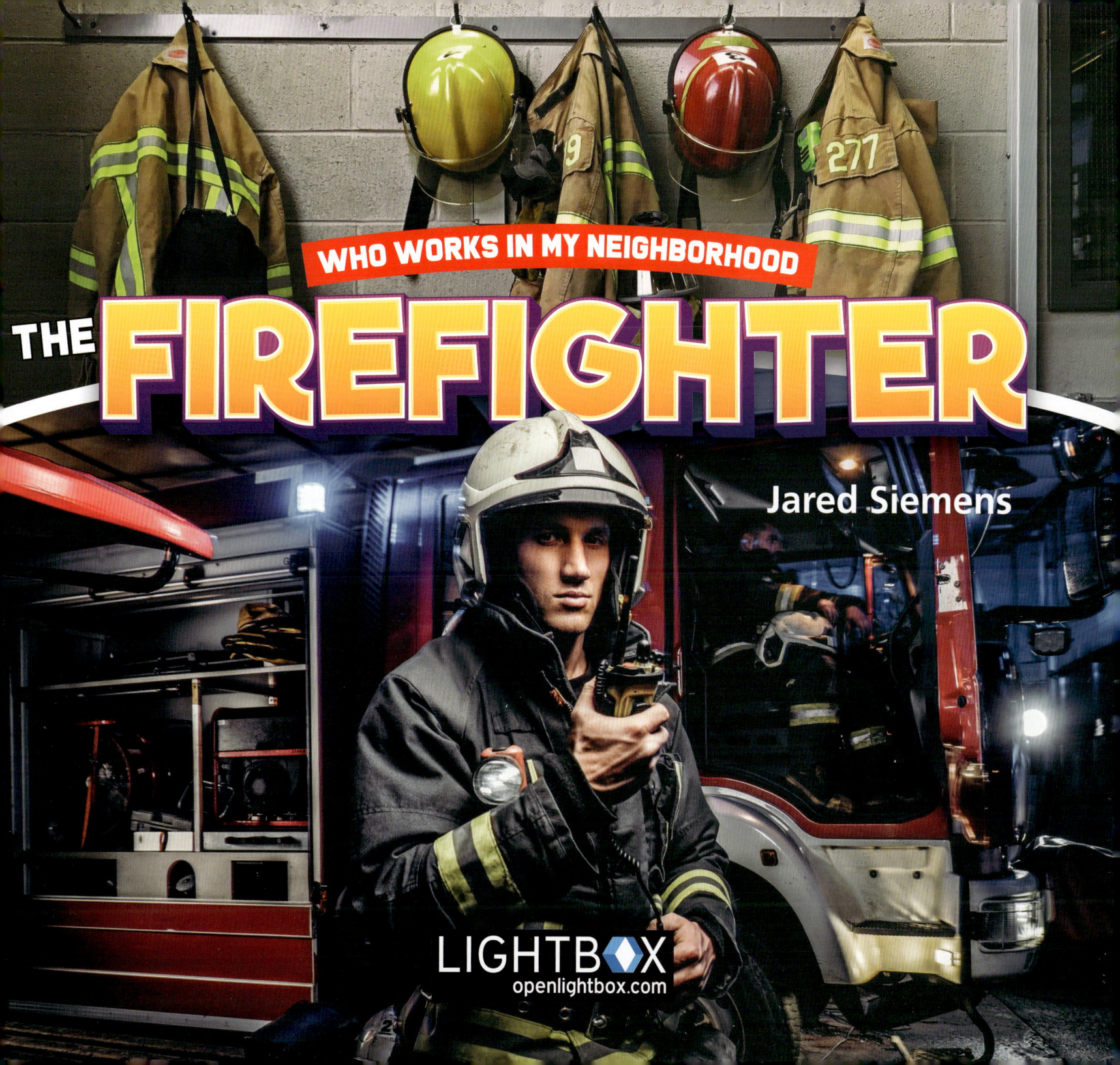

THE FIREFIGHTER

Jared Siemens

LIGHTBOX
openlightbox.com

LIGHTBOX

Go to
www.openlightbox.com
and enter this book's
unique code.

ACCESS CODE

LBXV7676

Lightbox is an all-inclusive digital solution for the teaching and learning of curriculum topics in an original, groundbreaking way. Lightbox is based on National Curriculum Standards.

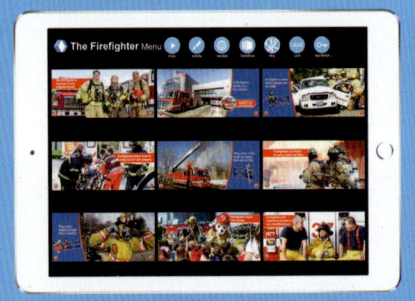

OPTIMIZED FOR
- ✓ TABLETS
- ✓ WHITEBOARDS
- ✓ COMPUTERS
- ✓ AND MUCH MORE!

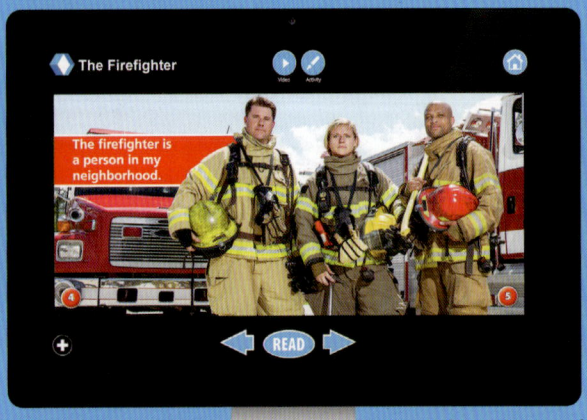

Copyright © 2021 Smartbook Media Inc. All rights reserved.

STANDARD FEATURES OF LIGHTBOX

AUDIO High-quality narration using text-to-speech system

VIDEOS Embedded high-definition video clips

ACTIVITIES Printable PDFs that can be emailed and graded

WEBLINKS Curated links to external, child-safe resources

SLIDESHOWS Pictorial overviews of key concepts

INTERACTIVE MAPS Interactive maps and aerial satellite imagery

QUIZZES Ten multiple choice questions that are automatically graded and emailed for teacher assessment

KEY WORDS Matching key concepts to their definitions

VIDEOS

WEBLINKS

SLIDESHOWS

QUIZZES

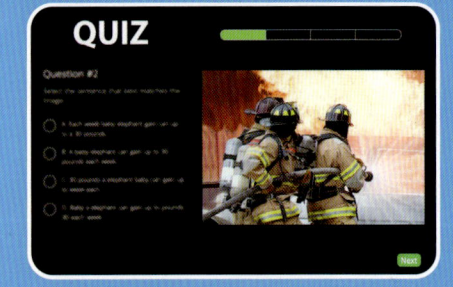

WHO WORKS IN MY NEIGHBORHOOD

THE FIREFIGHTER

Contents

2 Lightbox Access Code
4 The Firefighter
6 The Fire Station
8 Calling for Help
10 Helping the Hurt
12 Fire Trucks
14 Hoses
16 Masks
18 Fire Safety
20 My Neighborhood
22 Activity
24 Key Words

The firefighter is a person in my neighborhood.

5

6

A firefighter works at a fire station.

Los Angeles has the **busiest** fire station in the United States.

Firefighters come when people call for help.

There are more than **1 million** firefighters working in the **United States**.

9

10

Firefighters know how to help hurt or sick people.

11

12

They drive a fire truck to places that are on fire.

More than half of American firefighters are **volunteers**.

Firefighters use hoses to spray water on fires.

15

They wear masks to help them breathe.

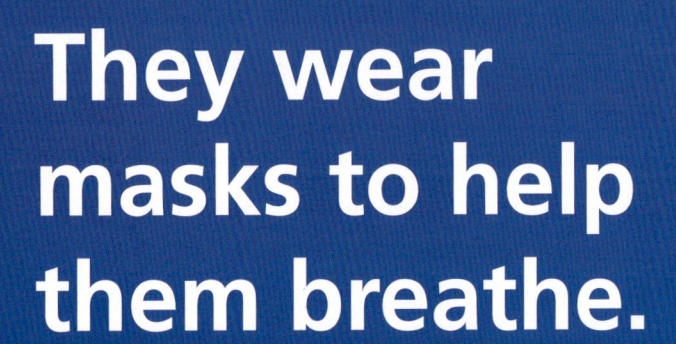

Firefighters wear about **60 pounds** of gear.

16

17

18

Firefighters teach fire safety.

19

Firefighters are important people in my neighborhood.

21

See what you have learned about the firefighter.

Describe what you see in each of the pictures.

23

KEY WORDS

Research has shown that as much as 65 percent of all written material published in English is made up of 300 words. These 300 words cannot be taught using pictures or learned by sounding them out. They must be recognized by sight. This book contains 33 common sight words to help young readers improve their reading fluency and comprehension. This book also teaches young readers several important content words, such as proper nouns. These words are paired with pictures to aid in learning and improve understanding.

Page	Sight Words First Appearance
4	a, in, is, my, the
7	at, has, state, works
8	are, call, come, for, help, more, people, than, there, when
11	how, know, or, to
13	of, on, places, that, they
14	use, water
16	about, them
20	important

Page	Content Words First Appearance
4	firefighter, neighborhood, person
7	fire station, Los Angeles, United States
11	hurt, sick
13	fire, fire truck, volunteers
14	hoses
16	gear, masks
19	safety

Published by Smartbook Media Inc.
350 5th Avenue, 59th Floor, New York, NY 10118
Website: www.openlightbox.com

Copyright ©2021 Smartbook Media Inc.
All rights reserved. No part of this publication may be reproduced, stored in a retrieval system, or transmitted in any form or by any means, electronic, mechanical, photocopying, recording, or otherwise, without the prior written permission of the publisher.

Library of Congress Control Number: 2020934522

ISBN 978-1-5105-5353-8 (hardcover)
ISBN 978-1-5105-5354-5 (multi-user eBook)

Printed in Guangzhou, China
1 2 3 4 5 6 7 8 9 0   24 23 22 21 20

042020
110819

Project Coordinator: Ryan Smith
Designer: Ana María Vidal

Every reasonable effort has been made to trace ownership and to obtain permission to reprint copyright material. The publisher would be pleased to have any errors or omissions brought to its attention so that they may be corrected in subsequent printings.

The publisher acknowledges Getty Images, Alamy, iStock, and Shutterstock as the primary image suppliers for this title.